Generis
PUBLISHING

Green Bonds In Emerging Economies: Critical Insights For Uganda's Transition To Climate Finance

JORUM DDUMBA

Title: **Green Bonds In Emerging Economies:**
Critical Insights For Uganda's Transition To Climate Finance

ISBN: 979-8-89966-464-9

Author: JORUM DDUMBA

Cover image: AI Generated

Publisher: Generis Publishing
Online orders: www.generis-publishing.com
Contact email: info@generis-publishing.com

GREEN BONDS IN EMERGING ECONOMIES: CRITICAL INSIGHTS FOR UGANDA'S TRANSITION TO CLIMATE FINANCE

Jorum Ddumba*, Camilla Shearman,

*Department of Environment & Natural Resources Management, Gulu University, P. O. Box 166, Gulu, Uganda.

Corresponding author: **Jorum Ddumba; Email: ddumbajorum5@gmail.com**

CONTENTS

ABSTRACT

Green bonds are increasingly recognized as innovative financial instruments for mobilizing capital to support climate change adaptation and mitigation. In Uganda, the transition to climate financing has become a critical component of efforts to achieve sustainable economic growth and address escalating climate-related challenges. Using a critical review methodology, this study synthesizes empirical research, financial records, and policy papers about Uganda's climate financing projects. This analysis is structured around global green finance standards, comparative insights from other emerging economies, and national legislation, including the Climate Change Act (2021), the Uganda Green Growth Development Strategy, and the National Development Plan III, as well as reports from the Ministry of Finance, Planning, and Economic Development (MoFPED). While Uganda's green bond framework remains in its early stages, it demonstrates significant potential. Initial efforts indicate that policy measures are well aligned with sustainable development objectives, especially in the areas of infrastructural resilience, sustainable agriculture, and renewable energy. Barriers such as institutional and regulatory gaps, underdeveloped capital markets, little and expensive transaction costs remain a challenge. Lessons learned from other African economies demonstrate the importance of clear certification procedures, effective credit improvement instruments, and regional collaboration in increasing issuance and uptake. Insights into how emerging economies can mobilize private capital for low-carbon development offers a valuable perspective on Uganda's transition to climate finance, including through the avenue of green bonds. Reforms should prioritize strengthening governance, ensuring compliance with global and national taxonomy and disclosure standards, and fostering local investor trust to enhance their effectiveness.

Keywords

Green bonds, Climate finance, Emerging economies, Sustainable development

Key policy highlights

- Uganda's transition to climate finance through green bonds requires robust governance and regulatory frameworks, including well defined institutional mandates and lower transaction costs.
- National guidelines must align with international taxonomies, disclosure requirements, and certification standards to strengthen credibility and attract investment.
- Expanding domestic capital markets and utilizing credit enhancement mechanisms will increase issuance volumes and market participation.
- Focused investor education, technical capacity development, and pilot demonstration projects are necessary to raise local investor awareness, mitigate perceived risks, and foster confidence in green financial instruments.
- Operationalisation of the National Green Taxonomy will support financers to identify eligible projects for a green bond and report against associated metrics.

INTRODUCTION

Developing countries are seeking new ways to finance the increasing costs of addressing climate change and preparing for its impacts (Liu & Paan, 2024). Finding financial resources for climate projects is now crucial because traditional funding sources are insufficient in volume to meet climate goals (Clark *et al.,* 2018). According to the Climate Policy Initiative report 2023, fighting climate change requires a significant amount of money; for example, recent estimates suggest that at least $6.2 trillion per year by 2030 is needed to meet the Paris Agreement goals. In this situation, green bonds have become a promising tool, letting governments and companies borrow money for environmental projects (Sun & Hao, 2025). The global green bond market has experienced rapid growth over the past decade (Adekoya, 2023). The amount of green bonds sold has increased: from $37 billion in 2014 to $633 billion in 2021, with a slight drop in 2022, followed by a rise to $620 billion in 2023 (Pava, 2024). This growth indicates that more investors are willing to invest in projects that benefit the environment, society, and that there is a strong demand for resilient infrastructure (Deschryver & de Mariz, 2020).

Emerging economies have begun to enter the green bond market, but their share remains relatively small compared to that of richer countries (Fatica *et al.,* 2021). Africa accounted for only approximately 0.3% of the total cumulative global green bond value and less than 1% of global issuances by number (FSDafrica,2025). According to the UNDP, by 2024, more than 15 African countries, including Egypt, Nigeria, Kenya, South Africa, Rwanda, Tanzania, and Gabon, helping to finance renewable energy and climate projects. Nigeria was the first African country to sell a government green bond in 2017, setting an example for others (Egwu et al., 2025). In 2019, Kenya issued East Africa's first green bond (KSh 4.3 billion/USD 33.3M) to fund environmentally friendly student housing (SFI, 2021). These first green bonds demonstrate the potential to attract funding from both domestic and international sources for climate projects in developing markets (Mohammed & Zadek, 2018). However, there remain challenges to the use of green bonds as a climate finance instrument, such as high transaction costs, incomplete rules and regulatory frameworks, and insufficient local investor participation (Mohammed & Zadek, 2018).

As a growing economy, Uganda intends to utilize green bonds as part of its plan to finance climate projects. The country is highly vulnerable to climate change and faces significant costs in transitioning to a cleaner economy that can better mitigate and adapt to climate-related problems (Verolme Hans, 2021). Uganda has addressed climate change by formulating policies, participating in international agreements including the UNFCCC, the Kyoto Protocol, and the Paris Agreement, and integrating green growth strategies into its national development frameworks.

Like other lower-middle income countries, Uganda has a funding gap of $28.1 billion to achieve its climate goals by 2030. This gap is evident in Uganda's climate plans, which heavily rely on external funding. (MWE,2022) Due to the limited size of public budgets and numerous other pressing development needs, Uganda is working to build its financial system to support sustainability and attract private investment. Green bonds are one of the new tools being considered to help close this funding gap (Pava, 2024).

Theoretical Framework

Green bonds are a crucial tool in sustainable finance, which aims to ensure that money is used in ways that benefit the environment. Green bonds are fixed-income securities - like conventional bonds, issuers such as governments, municipalities, banks, or companies borrow funds from investors and commit to repayment with interest (Hadaś-Dyduch et al., 2022). The key difference is that proceeds are destined to be used for environmentally sustainable projects. The International Capital Market Association's Green Bond Principles specify eligible projects, including renewable energy, energy efficiency, clean transportation, sustainable water management, climate-smart agriculture, forestry, biodiversity conservation, and pollution prevention (Napier *et al.,* 2025). Issuers must report on the all6ocation of funds and the environmental impact of their investments. This enhances transparency and accountability for investors (ICMA,

2025). The bonds attract investors who seek both financial returns and a positive environmental impact, which is part of a broader movement of Environmental, Social, and Governance (ESG) investing (Yu *et al., 2024*). By 2025, a total of over $6 trillion had been invested in green, social, sustainability, and sustainability-linked bonds (GSS+) worldwide. Green bonds enable investors to support climate-friendly projects without compromising on credit quality or returns (Bajra,2024). Most green bonds are backed by the issuer's promise to pay, so they have similar risks and returns as regular bonds from the same issuer (Khan & Vismara, 2025). This setup can attract more investors and sometimes lower the cost of borrowing for green projects, a benefit sometimes referred to as the green premium or 'greenium,' if investors are willing to accept slightly lower returns in exchange for environmental benefits (Wongaree et al., 2025). However, there is not enough clear evidence that a greenium always exists. Many green bonds are priced similarly to regular bonds, so the primary benefits are attracting more investors and enhancing reputation, rather than necessarily saving money on financing (Sun & Hao, 2025).

Green bonds may be structured in several forms. Some are backed by the issuer's overall finances, others are linked to specific projects, repaid from revenues generated by green initiatives, or secured by green assets (Khan & Vismara, 2025). The structure of a green bond is determined by the issuer's objectives and the characteristics of the underlying project (ADB, 2021). Government-issued and corporate green bonds have the potential to mobilize significant financial resources in countries such as Uganda, while smaller project bonds are more appropriate for targeted efforts, including the development of renewable energy systems (Pava, 2024). The central premise of green bonds is their ability to attract new capital, particularly from large private investors such as pension funds, insurance companies, and mutual funds seeking environmentally responsible investments. This mechanism can reduce the fiscal burden on governments (Fatica et al., 2021). Green bonds are also designed to finance projects that might not otherwise be implemented or to ensure that climate considerations are integrated into conventional infrastructure projects. Governments may promote green bonds to foster sustainable financial markets and to signal their commitment to climate objectives (Guesmi et al., 2025).

Greenwashing poses a significant risk if there are no robust regulations and effective monitoring. Some issuers might call their bonds 'green' without delivering significant positive environmental impacts, which can hurt trust in the market (Sneideriene & Legenzova, 2025). To mitigate this risk, markets should maintain clear lists of what constitutes green activities, provide tools and systems for effective monitoring aligned with national and global frameworks, and require external verification to ensure claims are accurate.

Research Objectives

i. To examine Uganda's Climate Finance Landscape
ii. To assess Green Bonds as a Climate Finance Instrument
iii. To analyze Challenges and Opportunities for Green Bond Adoption in Uganda

Uganda's Climate Finance Landscape

Uganda has gradually established a framework of policies to combat climate change and promote green growth, recognizing that the effects of climate change pose a threat to its long-term future (MoFPED,2025). To pave the way for a low-carbon and climate-resilient economy, the government enacted the National Climate Change Policy and its implementation strategy in 2015. Following this, Uganda submitted its first Nationally Determined Contribution (NDC) in 2016 as part of the Paris Agreement, including emissions reduction and adaptation strategies (MWE,2022). Targeting a conditional 22% reduction in emissions from business-as-usual by 2030, the first NDC was modest in scope and was projected to cost roughly $5.5 billion to achieve. Uganda pledged to provide 30% of the required funds locally, with the remaining 70% to be sourced from external assistance. Uganda has significantly raised its climate ambition since then. With the submission of an amended NDC in 2022, the mitigation target was increased to a 24.7% reduction by 2030 (economy-wide), and adaptation activities were expanded to encompass several industries (GGGI,2022). With an estimated USD 28.1 billion needed to fully implement Uganda's climate commitments by 2030, the new NDC has a hefty price tag (MWE,2022). Only a small portion (approximately 15%) of this is intended to be covered by unconditional, domestic funding, with the remaining amount to be covered by international finance. The majority ($17.5 billion) is designated for adaptation activities, and the remaining $10.4 billion is allocated for mitigation (MoFPED, 2024).

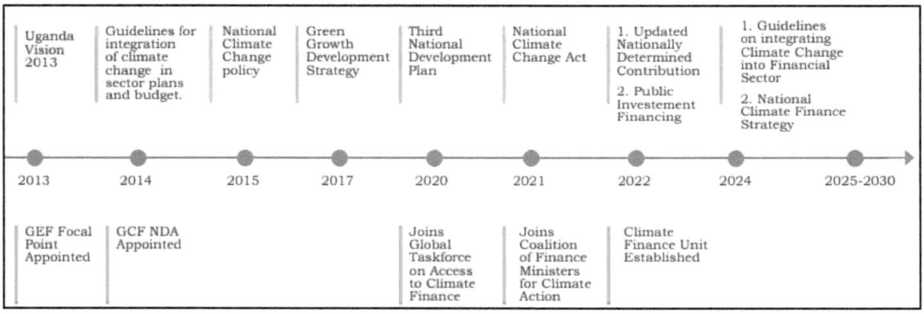

Figure 1. Timeline of Uganda's climate-related policy and strategy development, MoFPED, 2025

To operationalize its green growth vision, Uganda implemented the Uganda Green Growth Development Strategy (UGGDS) for the period 2017–18 to 2031, integrating green growth concepts into national planning (GGGI, 2022). Targeting key industries such as agriculture, energy, transportation, urbanization, and natural resources, the UGGDS emphasizes the importance of finance as a catalyst for implementation. It lists several funding sources for green growth, such as international climate funds, sustainable public procurement, green private company development, green taxation and subsidy reallocation, as well as public budget allocations. A combination of private sector investment, local revenue, and international climate funding is required. Uganda's national development plans have also mainstreamed climate and green growth. The Third National Development Plan (NDP III, 2020/21–2024/25) dedicates a comprehensive program to Climate Change, Natural Resources, Environment, and Water Management, aligning with the UGGDS (NPA, 2020). NDPIII acknowledges innovative financing mechanisms such as concessional loans, public-private partnerships, and green financing as key to funding Uganda's green growth priorities.

To enhance access to international climate finance, Uganda was the first African country to develop an NDC Partnership Plan in 2018, mobilizing support from various development partners (MWE,2022). Uganda has secured international climate funding for targeted projects, including grants from the Green Climate Fund (GCF) and the Global Environment Facility (GEF). These resources have been obtained through accredited entities such as the United Nations Development Programme (UNDP), the Food and Agriculture Organization (FAO), and GEF partner agencies, including the United Nations Environment Programme (UNEP).However, navigating these funding mechanisms can be complex (Bakiika, 2020). In recent years, the Ugandan government has taken notable steps to strengthen its domestic climate finance governance and attract new forms of finance: Uganda enacted a Climate Change Act (2021) that, among other provisions, formalizes climate change coordination mechanisms and could provide a basis for climate finance. With assistance from partners including Global Green Growth Institute (GGGI) and the UK Foreign, Commonwealth, and Development Office, the Ministry of Finance, Planning, and Economic Development (MoFPED) created a special Climate Finance Unit (CFU) in 2021 (MoFPED, 2025). The mission of the CFU is to explore innovative financing options and establish a pipeline of bankable climate initiatives. This unit is actively building capacity across government and sectors on climate finance and working to integrate climate considerations into budgeting processes. Uganda also finalized a National Climate Finance Strategy as of 2025. This will provide a financial roadmap that supports Uganda's Green Growth Development Strategy and describes how the country plans to raise, distribute, and monitor climate funds from many sources. Instruments such as climate funds, blended finance, and green bonds are likely included in this strategy's solution mix. To "green" the public financial management system, Uganda has introduced a Climate Budget Tagging system (CBT), a tool to label and track climate-related expenditures across government budgets, thereby improving transparency and enabling the government to monitor its spending on climate objectives (Navarro, 2024). This can also help in reporting to international partners and in making the case for an influx of additional international climate finance.

Uganda developed a green finance taxonomy in 2023–2024. A green taxonomy defines which economic activities qualify as environmentally sustainable (or 'green') within a national context (MOFPED, 2025). By providing investors and financial institutions with clarity on what constitutes a "green" project, Uganda's creation of this framework paves the way for the issuance of green bonds, reporting and aggregation of impact indicators at a national level, and the prevention of greenwashing (Bhattacharyya,2021). The taxonomy is expected to be utilized by banks, corporations, and governmental entities to identify green projects and align investments with national climate objectives. Uganda established a National Climate Finance Vehicle in 2023, which is effectively a trust fund with many donors that is managed by MoFPED. The goal of this vehicle is to combine funds from carbon markets, international climate funds (such as the Green Climate Fund (GCF) and Global Environment Facility (GEF), and other contributors into a single fund that may subsequently be used to invest in national climate goals. The NCFV can blend grants with other financing and provide a coordinated mechanism to channel funds to projects, possibly improving efficiency and scale. If operationalized effectively, this could also co-finance or credit-enhance green bond projects in the future (Ogunsola *et.al.,*2024) and provide leverage for public finance by crowding in and catalysing private sector investment.

There is increasing emphasis on involving Uganda's private sector in climate finance. The government and Uganda Development Bank (UDB) highlighted the vulnerability of key industries and the need for private investment in climate adaptation for sectors like agriculture and MSMEs. Uganda's financial institutions are being encouraged to develop green financial products such as Equity Bank's Equi green loan (UBA,2024). Some initiatives, such as the Agricultural Credit Facility at the Bank of Uganda and the Yield Uganda impact investment fund, are geared towards sustainable agriculture and renewable energy. Through these measures, Uganda is gradually building an ecosystem that can support climate finance flows. However, critical challenges remain with domestic financial institutions, which often have high lending rates, making local debt expensive; the financial sector's ability to appraise fund and report on green projects is limited by technical capacity and perceived risks; and as of 2025, much of Uganda's climate finance still comes from external public sources such as grants/loans rather than private investment (MoFPED, 2025).

Green Bonds as a Climate Finance Instrument

As of mid-2025, no green bonds (public or corporate) have been officially issued in Uganda. A recent Climate Policy Initiative report confirms that "to date, Uganda has not seen clear issuances of green bonds (MoFPED, 2025). The closest example was a thematic corporate bond issued by Kakira Sugar Limited bond in 2013 of UGX 76 billion (USD 30 million) corporate bond. The Kakira bond, which at the time was not known as a "green bond," was used to fund the development of sugar production, including a bagasse-based cogeneration power plant that offered environmental benefits (Lab Instrument Analysis, 2024). This shows that Uganda's private sector has experience issuing bonds for sustainable development-aligned projects, even in the absence of a regulated green bond market. Significant groundwork is being laid to make green bond financing a reality, and in the past few years, the idea of issuing green bonds has gained traction within government circles and among development partners as part of a broader strategy to mobilize climate finance (Pava, 2024) (Olawale Adisa *et al.,* 2024).

Uganda's Ministry of Finance (MoFPED) has recognised the potential of green bonds to spur climate change resilience and mitigation (MoFPED, 2025). After reviewing several instruments, the Deutsche Gesellschaft für Internationale Zusammenarbeit (GIZ) analysed that results-based financing, carbon markets, debt-for-nature swaps, SME green finance, and green bonds were Uganda's top priorities (Verolme Hans, 2021). With support from the EU, a second study specifically assessed the feasibility of issuing green bonds in Uganda and concluded that certain preparations were necessary, including the development of a national green taxonomy and a framework for green bonds. To attract more investors, the study also expressed its support for the expansion of Uganda's green bond market and stated that it would be open to acting as an anchor investor for the nation's first green bond. In a new market, this outside support is essential for fostering confidence (Riaz *et al.,* 2025).

In 2023, the Ugandan Capital Markets Authority (CMA) initiated the development of a legal framework for green bonds. To promote green financing, the CMA's Strategic Development Plan recommends collaborating with organizations such as the EU-funded Uganda Green Enterprise Finance Accelerator (UGEFA) and revising corporate bond regulations to include green bond provisions (CMA, 2023). Regulatory recognition is a step in the right direction, even though exact criteria are still being developed. Other African countries, such as Kenya, Nigeria, Morocco, and Rwanda, have introduced green bond guidelines (Ngwenya & Simatele, 2020), and Uganda is following suit to ensure that any green bond issuance meets international best practices, including alignment with the International Capital Market Association (ICMA) Green Bond Principles and the Climate Bonds Standard. A key enabler now in place is the Uganda Green Taxonomy (completed in 2023), which defines eligible green projects in the Ugandan context. This taxonomy will inform the criteria for green bond use-of-proceeds and help both issuers and investors identify qualifying projects such as renewable energy installations, sustainable agriculture projects, or green transport infrastructure in Uganda (MoFPED, 2025). The country is working on generating a pipeline of projects suitable for green financing. Sectors ripe for green bond financing in Uganda include renewable energy (solar), small hydro, climate-smart agriculture and agroforestry, energy-efficient buildings, public transport, and resilient water infrastructure, all of which could be funded by green bond proceeds if projects are structured appropriately.

Uganda can issue a green bond under the structures below:

A sovereign green bond issued by the Government of Uganda through the Ministry of Finance, Planning and Economic Development (MoFPED) could raise funds for public green projects, following the example set by Nigeria. However, considering Uganda's current debt levels and borrowing costs, such an issuance may require credit enhancement or concessional financing elements.

A corporate green bond could be issued by a state-owned enterprise or a private company. For instance, the Uganda Electricity Generation Company or the National Water and Sewerage Corporation could issue green bonds to finance renewable energy plants or water treatment facilities. Additionally, large banks could issue green bonds to provide financing for green projects through on-lending.

Multilateral development banks or Development Finance Institutions (DFIs), such as the East African Development Bank or the African Development Bank, could issue regional green bonds and allocate a portion of the proceeds to projects in Uganda. However, such an approach would not be classified as a Ugandan green bond issuance.

A municipal green bond could be considered; however, Uganda's local governments currently lack the fiscal autonomy required to access capital markets.

Table 1. Structures of Green bonds issued by some of the African Countries

Country / Issuer	Year(s)	Structure of Bond	Purpose
Nigeria (Government)	2017	Sovereign	Renewable energy, afforestation, transport
Seychelles	2018	Sovereign	Marine conservation, fisheries (Blue Bond)
Egypt	2020	Sovereign	clean transport/energy/water projects
Access Bank (Nigeria)	2019	Corporate	Energy efficiency, renewables, agriculture
North South Power	2019	Corporate	Green power infrastructure
OneWattSolar (Nigeria)	2021	Corporate	Off-grid solar (Green Sukuk)
Cape Town (South Africa)	2017	Municipal	Water infrastructure, flood protection
Johannesburg (South Africa)	2013	Municipal	Climate change response projects
Tanga (Tanzania)	2024	Municipal	Water supply expansion, smart meters
AfDB	Ongoing	Multilateral development bank	Pan-African green infrastructure & energy

Modified from, Olawale,2024; Banga, 2019; Ngwenya,2020 & Cheteni,2024

With training for financial sector participants on climate risks and project planning, the Climate Finance Unit's efforts to increase capacity are starting to yield results. Additionally, creative pilot transactions are being created. For example, the Invest HER Climate Resilience Bond, a proposed private sector-led bond, intends to finance climate-smart, women-led agribusinesses in Uganda (Lab Instrument Analysis, 2024). Despite still being in the early stages of development, this instrument is positioned as Uganda's first gender-focused green bond, with the goal of being partially guaranteed by development partners and issued in local currency. Such a pilot could demonstrate the viability of green bonds in Uganda and help build market confidence.

While Uganda has not yet issued a green bond, the building blocks of policy commitment, regulatory framework in progress, project pipeline development, and stakeholder interest are being assembled. The real test will be moving from plans to execution, and ensuring that when a green bond is launched, it is met with sufficient demand.

Challenges and Opportunities for Green Bond Adoption

The key challenges that Uganda faces in leveraging green bonds, as well as the opportunities that make green bonds an attractive proposition, are discussed below. Understanding both sides is crucial for policymakers and stakeholders as they chart a path forward (Sajid *et al.,* 2024).

Challenges

Uganda's financial markets are small and not yet well-equipped for sophisticated instruments (CMA, 2017). The government bond market (Treasury bonds) is active but dominated by short to medium maturities and a handful of investors, mainly local banks, the National Social Security Fund (NSSF), and some foreign investors seeking high yields (IMF, 2024). Corporate bond issuances have been few: other than the Kakira bond and a few bank issuances in the early 2010s, there has not been a vibrant corporate bond market (USE, 2020). The Capital Markets Authority of Uganda categorized the market as "narrow and underdeveloped, with limited product offerings and a narrow investor base reliant on foreign investments. This can hinder the adoption of a new instrument, such as green bonds. Low liquidity and shallow secondary market mean investors may be reluctant to buy and hold Ugandan green bonds unless compensated with higher yields.

This context implies that a Ugandan green bond may need to attract non-traditional investors, such as international climate-focused funds, or offer additional incentives to domestic investors. Uganda has institutional investors, notably the National Social Security Fund and insurance companies, which manage sizable assets and seek stable, long-term investments. Their demand for green bonds can be increased through a combination of investment-grade credit enhancements or guarantees, competitive risk-adjusted yields with predictable cash flows, and transparent regulatory and tax incentives. These measures should be supported by credible verification and reporting processes that mitigate the risk of greenwashing.

Prevailing interest rates in Uganda are high, commercial lending rates averaging at 21%, and government bond yields in the mid-teens (Lukoye, 2025). Yields on 10-year Ugandan government bonds often range from 15% to 17% in recent years, reflecting inflation and credit risk (USE, 2024). Such highly required returns could make green bond financing expensive for issuers, potentially affecting the benefit of attracting capital. Unless concessional elements are introduced, a green bond may not offer any more favorable terms than a conventional bond issuance. Conversely, this situation presents an opportunity to attract foreign capital through green bonds. For example, Germany's 10-year green bond yields are closely aligned with its conventional Bund yields, remaining near 2.8% in early 2026. Additionally, the 2033 green bond yielded approximately 2.16% in late 2024.

Uganda's public debt and fiscal deficit levels constrain its borrowing headroom (Wanyenya, 2025). Taking on a sovereign green bond adds debt stock, even if for a good purpose. There is a risk of over-leveraging if not managed prudently. Moreover, currency risk looms large; a bond denominated in local currency might deter foreigners, whereas a bond denominated in a foreign currency exposes Uganda to exchange rate volatility.

Although there has been some progress, Uganda currently **lacks a fully tested green bond regulatory framework**. Draft rules and regulations for green bonds are available as of 2025. It takes more work to reassure investors when there are no track record or local standards. Furthermore, aligning local frameworks with international norms so that global investors are comfortable is an ongoing task (Ntambirweki, 2022). Many stakeholders, ranging from government agencies to financial institutions, are new to structuring and managing green finance (Blum, 2024). There are capacity gaps in project preparation, environmental risk assessment, and monitoring of proceedings. This raises implementation risk. For example, without capacity, reporting might be inadequate, particularly for use of proceeds, there may not be enough pipeline reporting to fulfil the requirements this is a common issue, as indicated by the Luxembourg Green Stock Exchange, which could damage credibility.

Having **sufficient bankable green projects** is a challenge. Many climate projects in Uganda are small or dispersed such as off-grid solar installations, community water projects, and require varying sizes of investment. This can increase transaction costs of sourcing projects for the pipeline, thereby increasing costs of the bond. Packaging these into a sizeable bond issuance is complex. Small issue sizes also face investor skepticism regarding liquidity and impact (Verolme Hans, 2021). Developing portfolios of bankable green projects, particularly within the micro, small, and medium enterprise (MSME) sector, is essential. Although ticket sizes and MSME activities differ, standard green technologies or investments along shared value chains can be identified and aggregated for green bond issuance.

Domestic investor awareness of green bonds is currently low. Institutions such as pension funds may not yet have ESG mandates or the necessary knowledge to evaluate green investments. Similarly, the general investing public is unfamiliar with green bonds. This could initially limit local demand, and a heavy reliance on a few foreign investors could be precarious. There is also the question of whether investors strongly believe in the "green" aspect to participate; any suspicion of greenwashing could diminish demand (Rozkov, 2023). In the absence of strong procedures, it is possible that funds will inadvertently support initiatives with dubious green credentials, such as designating something green when there is no clear and substantial positive impact on the environment (Monaco, 2025). This danger highlights the need for rigorous control and independent verification on environmental indicators, a novel endeavor for many Ugandan auditors, financial institutions, and regulators.

If Uganda's strategy is to rely on anchor investors or guarantees from development partners, any **delay or change in commitment from those partners** could derail a planned issuance.

Opportunities

Green bonds can play an important role in **catalysing private sector finance for green growth**, both domestic investors and international investors. (Pava, 2024). Given the enormous disparity between the current funding and the demands for climate finance, catalysing private sector investment is crucial (Vu *et al.,*2025). Internationally, green bonds offer a chance to access international ESG investor funds looking for emerging market impact potential.

Domestically, green bonds can **keep domestic savings invested in domestically productive, green ventures**, rather than solely in government treasuries or overseas assets. According to the Economic Policy Research Centre report 2018, Uganda's pension funds, insurance companies, and banks could play a bigger role in financing development. Green bonds provide these institutions with a tailored product that matches their long-term liabilities with long-term, sustainable assets (Della *et al.,* 2011). For instance, the National Social Security Fund could invest in a government-backed green bond to support national solar power projects.

Uganda's pursuit of innovative climate finance instruments, like green bonds, has garnered **international goodwill**. Development partners have demonstrated a readiness to assist, as seen in the EU's willingness to act as an anchor investor (OECD, 2023). Such support can de-risk the initial transactions. Successful issuance would enhance Uganda's reputation as a climate finance pioneer among Least Developed Countries, potentially leading to more technical and financial support from climate funds and investors for subsequent projects (MoFPED, 2025).

The preparation for green bonds has **positive externalities for governance and coordination**. It has driven the creation of a green taxonomy and improved coordination between finance and environmental authorities. Over time, these improvements in governance and capacity will benefit Uganda's overall public investment management. Climate budget tagging and the climate finance strategy are being strengthened in tandem, meaning green bonds are part of a holistic enhancement of how climate action is financed and tracked in Uganda (OECD, 2021).

A successful green bond could have a **catalytic effect on attracting more investors into Uganda's capital market** (Cheng, 2024). It introduces new product innovations that can attract more participants. If issued in local currency, it could encourage more Ugandans to invest (perhaps through green retail savings bonds) and build a culture of sustainable investing. According to the OECD, 2025 study issuing bonds in local currency and involving local investors can strengthen local capital markets and diversify the investor base (Pointek, 2025). This aligns with Uganda's goal of reducing over-reliance on foreign portfolio investors and building domestic financial resilience.

By financing green infrastructure, green bonds can help Uganda **achieve NDC targets through emission reductions and increased resilience** while also spurring economic growth and job creation in green industries. Investments in areas such as renewable energy, climate-smart agriculture, and green transportation tend to have multiplier effects (Farag, 2014). They create jobs, reduce energy costs, and improve public health through reduced pollution (Simionescu, 2024). This supports Uganda's sustainable development and Vision 2040 goals, moving the country towards a greener economy.

Green bonds in Uganda need not stand alone; they can be part of **blended finance structures to make green investments bankable**. For example, a tranche of a green bond could be taken up by concessional investors, such as a development bank, at lower returns, effectively subsidizing the overall cost and allowing market investors to participate with reduced risk. Blended finance can thus make borderline projects bankable. By directing climate fund funds into a junior tranche and so leveraging more private finance at senior levels, Uganda's Climate Finance Vehicle may be able to offer this kind of assistance. With this opportunity, Uganda may optimize its capital stack for climate initiatives by utilizing green bonds as a vehicle for aggregating funds from multiple sources.

If Uganda manages to issue a green bond, it will join a small but growing cohort of African nations that have done so (FSD Africa, 2025). This could position Uganda as a leader among low-income countries in innovative finance (Nanyonjo, 2024). There is an opportunity to share lessons with other countries in East Africa or the NDC Partnership community, **enhancing Uganda's diplomatic and technical clout in climate negotiations**. It may also open avenues for regional projects such as an East African green bond for a cross-border renewable energy project with Uganda's participation.

Unlocking the potential of green bonds for Uganda will require strategic action to mitigate risks. Careful design, including ensuring credit enhancement, strong project selection, and effective investor engagement, can address many challenges. The opportunities are compelling not only for raising funds but also for the broader, positive impacts on Uganda's financial system and sustainable development trajectory.

Methodology

A qualitative critical review design, supplemented by comparative case study analysis, was used to examine Uganda's emerging experience with green bonds. The analysis focuses on Uganda's climate finance ecosystem by assessing institutional preparedness, identifying potential sectors for green bond financing such as renewable energy, sustainable agriculture, water, and climate-resilient infrastructure, and evaluating the national policy and regulatory framework, including the Climate Change Act (2021), the Green Growth Development Strategy, and the National Development Plan III. Data were primarily obtained from secondary sources, including government policy documents, reports from the World Bank, AfDB, UNDP, FSD Africa, and the Climate Bonds Initiative, peer-reviewed literature, and green bond issuance databases. Data collection included documentary review and cross-country benchmarking of African issuances in Kenya, Rwanda, Tanzania, Nigeria, South Africa, and Seychelles.

Ethical standards were upheld by focusing on publicly available data to ensure transparency and replicability.

Results and Discussion

Table 2. East Africa's Green Bond Issuance

Country	Issuer / Instrument	Year	Amount	Remarks	References
Kenya	Acorn Holdings – Corporate Green Bond (Tranche 1)	2019	KES 4.3bn (~US$40m)	First certified green bond in Kenya/East Africa; funds for six purpose-built, EDGE-aligned student housing projects in Nairobi; listed on Nairobi Stock Exchange (NSE) and London Stock Exchange (LSE); partially guaranteed by FSD Africa	SFI,2021
Kenya	Acorn Holdings – Green Bond (Tranche 2, MTN upsizing)	2021	KES 2.096bn	Oversubscribed (146%); adds two more green-certified student housing sites.	Acorn,2021
Rwanda	Prime Energy Plc – Corporate Green Bond	2024	RWF 9.58bn (~US$7.06m)	7-year bond; ~79% allocated to the 10 MW Rukarara VI run-of-river hydropower project, remainder for maintaining existing small hydro plants; listed on RSE; fully subscribed. Prime energy Ltd.	Rusera,2023
Tanzania	Tanga UWASA –	2024	~US$20.8m (TZS)	Tanzania's first sub-national green bond; finances water	Malika,2025

Sub-national Green Bond		production increase, 60 km network extension, smart meters, loss reduction; listed on DSE & Luxembourg Green Exchange; 103% oversubscribed. UNCDF

The green bond market in East Africa is expanding, with Kenya, Rwanda, and Tanzania emerging as leading participants, while Uganda remains in the preparatory phase. Acorn Holdings' corporate green bonds, issued in 2019 and 2021, set a benchmark for Kenya; both issuances were oversubscribed, demonstrating strong investor demand and highlighting the importance of credit guarantees in building market confidence (Acorn, 2021). Rwanda's Prime Energy Plc introduced a corporate green bond in 2024 to finance small hydropower projects, further illustrating the region's commitment to sustainable finance (Rusera, 2023).

In 2024, Tanga Urban Water Supply and Sanitation Authority (UWASA) in Tanzania issued the region's first sub-national green bond, which focused on water resilience and achieved oversubscription, reflecting strong investor confidence (Malika, 2025).

OTHER GREEN/BLUE BOND ISSUANCES IN AFRICA

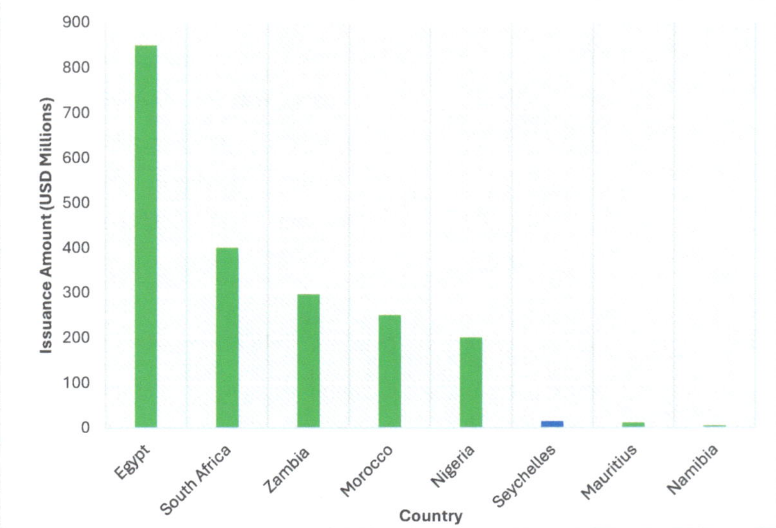

Figure 3. Other green/blue bond issuances in Africa

Egypt is the largest issuer of green bonds in Africa. In September 2020, Egypt issued the continent's largest internationally listed sovereign green bond, valued at US$750 million, as well as a US$100 million corporate green bond from Commercial International Bank (CIB). The proceeds were allocated to clean transportation projects, such as Cairo Metro expansions, as well as renewable energy, sustainable water and sanitation systems, and pollution reduction initiatives (IFC, 2022).

South Africa was the first country in Africa to issue a green bond, with the City of Johannesburg launching a municipal green bond in 2014. This was followed by Cape Town's water-focused bond in 2017 and corporate issuances, including Nedbank's renewable energy bonds (DFFE, 2022).

Zambia, through the Copperbelt Energy Corporation (2024), raised capital for the Itimpi Solar Power Station project.

Morocco has participated actively in the green bond market through agencies such as the Moroccan Agency for Sustainable Energy (MASEN), which issued bonds for solar energy projects. Additionally, banks and real estate developers have issued corporate green and sustainability bonds (Farhad *et.al*, 2022).

Nigeria was the first African sovereign to issue a green bond in 2017, followed by subsequent tranches to finance renewable energy, afforestation, and clean transport projects (Egwu et al., 2025).

The Seychelles Blue Bond (2018) is a notable example, as it financed marine conservation and sustainable fisheries, representing the first bond of its kind.

Mauritius, through EnVolt, issued a Green Project Bond (2023) for the construction of solar roof and ground-mounted facilities across the island (MCB group Sustainability Report 2024).

Bank Windhoek in Namibia pioneered the first green bond issuance in Southern Africa outside of South Africa (Green Bond Impact Report 2020).

A review of the issued green bonds in African countries show some critical success factors that can be considered for Uganda's green bond development. The critical success factors further address challenges and opportunities outlined above:

1. **Clarity and alignment of policy, regulatory frameworks and taxonomies are fundamental**

   Experience across African markets shows that green bond issuance is more successful where there is clear policy guidance, defined regulatory frameworks, and alignment with recognised standards. South Africa's early adoption of green bond listing rules in 2017 and aligning with international principles helped build investor confidence, while Zambia's initial difficulties due to the absence of guidelines underscore the importance of regulatory clarity. Once green bond guidelines were introduced, Zambia's subsequent issuance in 2023 achieved a 178% oversubscription.

   At the global level, fragmented definitions of what constitutes "green" have emerged as a recurring challenge. The existence of more than 30 green taxonomies worldwide has increased transaction costs and created uncertainty for cross-border investors. The European Union's experience is instructive: Prior to 2023, the absence of a harmonised green bond standard in the European Union contributed to market fragmentation. The adoption of the European Green Bond Standard (EU GBS), with a mandatory link to the EU Taxonomy for sustainable activities, reflects a shift towards greater consistency and comparability. This suggests that early attention to taxonomy alignment and interoperability may help avoid fragmentation as Uganda's market develops.

2. **Blended finance and de-risking mechanisms increase viability.**
   Kenya's Acorn Green Bond certified by the Climate Bonds Initiative was supported with a partial guarantee on 50% of the principal and interest by GuarantCo, a Private Infrastructure Development Group company. This improved the risk profile of the bond and contributed to its success.

3. **Certification boosts credibility.**
   Independent verification and certification have proven to be central to building trust in green bond markets. Certification by recognised entities, such as the Climate Bonds Initiative, helps reassure investors regarding the environmental integrity of the bond and reduces concerns about greenwashing. The Lagos State sub-national green bond, which issued certification before pricing, illustrates how early external validation can enhance market confidence.

   Across global and EU markets, robust disclosure on use of proceeds and impact reporting has similarly been associated with stronger investor demand and reputational resilience.

4. **Diversification enhances impact.**
   Beyond renewable energy and energy efficiency, diverse use of proceeds towards other green sectors such as green housing, biodiversity, blue economy can enhance impact. The Seychelles Blue Bond highlights how thematic diversification can mobilise capital for sectors that are otherwise underfinanced.

Another form of diversification could come through developing a Sustainability Bond that integrates other impact areas, for example social inclusion and gender. Sustainability Bonds have use of proceeds for environmental and social impact indicators, which could support Uganda to develop projects that ensure the inclusion of women, youth and other marginalised groups.

5. **Institutional capacity and public-sector leadership shape market outcomes**

   Limited institutional capacity has frequently constrained green bond development, particularly in relation to project pipelines, reporting requirements, and compliance with standards. Countries that invested in capacity building for regulators, issuers, and market participants have generally been better positioned to sustain issuance over time.

   Public-sector leadership has also played a catalytic role. Sovereign, municipal, or development bank issuances have often acted as anchor transactions, helping establish benchmarks, build market familiarity, and signal long-term commitment to sustainable finance.

   For example, under the EU's NextGenerationEU (NGEU) programme, the European Commission emerged as a large-scale green bond issuer, supported by significant investment in institutional systems to track, allocate and report on taxonomy-aligned expenditures across member states. This public-sector leadership helped establish market benchmarks, normalise high standards of transparency, and catalyse broader green bond issuance across the EU. A comparable dynamic can be observed in Nigeria, where the Federal Government's sovereign green bond issuances from 2017 onwards required capacity building across government institutions to manage project selection and reporting. These sovereign issuances played a catalytic role in demonstrating feasibility, strengthening market confidence, and stimulating interest in subsequent sub-national and corporate green bond activity.

Conclusion

In the context of limited local resources and multiple market constraints, Uganda's green bonds illustrate the broader challenges encountered by developing countries in mobilizing funds for climate action. This initiative provides important insights for other nations facing similar circumstances. Uganda's strategy is marked by deliberate planning, institution-building, and the adoption of innovative solutions. The success of green bonds in Uganda depends on their careful execution and continuous backing from both local and foreign partners. By financing resilient infrastructure, clean energy, and other ecologically friendly initiatives that support economic growth, green bonds have the potential to significantly advance Uganda's sustainable development.

A green bond could expedite Uganda's green initiatives and send a message to the world that the country is committed to sustainable development if it is properly planned and supported. However, if hurried or badly designed, a green bond may perform poorly or deter investors. The success factors will include ensuring robust project pipelines, possibly securing partial guarantees or concessional components, investor outreach and education to familiarize local investors with green bonds, and maintaining strong transparency standards. Whether green bonds become a game-changing component of Uganda's climate financing conundrum or remain a theoretical idea will depend on how well they can address their issues, which range from market depth to technical capabilities.

Recommendations

Given the risks, Uganda can consider a **pilot green bond of a moderate size**, supported by guarantees or anchor investment from development partners. This pilot could be a sovereign green bond tied to a few investment-ready projects, such as a solar PV park and a climate-smart agriculture program to showcase viability. Alternatively, supporting a corporate entity or municipality, such as Kampala City, in issuing a green bond with partial guarantee could also demonstrate the concept.

A digital platform that identifies, standardizes, and aggregates potential green projects for bond financing is recommended. The platform would follow an approved green taxonomy, implement uniform eligibility criteria for all projects, automate documentation and pre-issuance verification, and produce a validated list of projects eligible for bond issuance. This strategy is anticipated to improve transparency and comparability among issuers and sectors, lower due diligence and structuring costs, expedite issuance, and encourage increased participation from institutional investors and other market participants.

Uganda's establishment of a Climate Finance Unit and its collaboration with expert partners, such as GGGI and the NDC Partnership, among others, illustrates the importance of **building local capacity**. A recommendation is for Uganda to continue training personnel in ministries, banks, and capital market institutions on green finance, and to engage experienced underwriters or advisors for the first issuance. Knowledge exchange with countries that have issued green bonds such as Egypt, Nigeria, Kenya, Rwanda, among others could be beneficial.

Over time, Uganda can aim to create a sustainable pipeline of green bonds. This could involve standardizing green criteria across projects through the National Green Taxonomy, encouraging banks to lend to green projects, perhaps bundling those loans into asset-backed green securities, and even exploring regional green bond issuances to achieve scale.

Strict rules pertaining to transparency and effective reporting must be followed by every green bond issued by Uganda. By doing this, it will ensure that the instrument meets its environmental obligations and maintains its stakeholders' trust. Using third-party verifiers or forming an independent monitoring committee for Uganda's green bonds are two possible strategies to increase credibility.

Ethical Compliance

The research did not involve human participants however other ethical standards of the institutional and/or national research committee were adhered to.

Funding

This research did not receive any form of funding.

Disclosure statement

The authors report there are no competing interests to declare

REFERENCES

Acorn. 2021. "Final Tranche of Acorn Green Bond Oversubscribed." https://acornholdingsafrica.com/wp-content/uploads/2021/07/Press-Release-Final-Tranche-of-Green-Bond.pdf.

Adisa, Olawale, Bamidele Segun Ilugbusi, Ogugua Chimezie Obi, Kehinde Feranmi Awonuga, and Onyeka Franca Asuzu. 2024. "Green Bonds in Climate Finance: A Review of USA and African Initiatives." *International Journal of Science and Research Archive* 11 (1): 2376–2383. https://doi.org/10.30574/ijsra.2024.11.1.0147.

Bajra, Ujkan Q., and Niklas Wagner. 2024. "Analyzing the Impact of Eco-friendly Bonds on Economic Growth and Environmental Sustainability." *Borsa Istanbul Review* 24 (4): 722–731. https://doi.org/10.1016/j.bir.2024.04.003.

Bakiika, R., C. Mbatuusa, A. Mugeere, and A. Amumpiire. 2020. "Climate Finance Mobilization in Uganda: The Most Viable Financing Option." *Policy Research* Paper Series No. 102. Kampala: ACODE.

Banga, Josué. 2019. "The Green Bond Market: A Potential Source of Climate Finance for Developing Countries." *Journal of Sustainable Finance and Investment* 9 (1): 17–32. https://doi.org/10.1080/20430795.2018.1498617.

Bhattacharyya, Rupsha. 2021. "Green Finance for Energy Transition, Climate Action and Sustainable Development: Overview of Concepts, Applications, Implementation and Challenges." *Green Finance* 4 (1): 1–35. https://doi.org/10.3934/GF.2022001.

Blum, S. 2024. "UGEFA Case Study—Green Finance Developments in Uganda". Berlin: Adelphi Research gGmbH. https://sun-connect.org/wp-content/uploads/UGEFA-Case-Study_Green-Finance-Developments-in-Uganda.pdf.

Capital Markets Authority (CMA). 2017. *Capital Markets Development Master Plan.* Kampala: Capital Markets Authority. https://cmauganda.co.ug/capital-markets-development-master-plan/.

Cheng, G., T. Ehlers, F. Packer, and Y. Xiao. 2024. "Sovereign Green Bonds: A Catalyst for Sustainable Debt Market Development." *IMF Working Papers* (120): A001. Accessed Oct 18, 2025. https://doi.org/10.5089/9798400277030.001.A001.

Clark, Robyn, James Reed, and Terry Sunderland. 2018. "Bridging Funding Gaps for Climate and Sustainable Development: Pitfalls, Progress and Potential of Private Finance." *Land Use Policy* 71: 335–346. https://doi.org/10.1016/j.landusepol.2017.12.013.

Della Croce, Raffaele, Christopher Kaminker, and Fiona Stewart. 2011. *The Role of Pension Funds in Financing Green Growth Initiatives.* OECD Working Papers on Finance, Insurance and Private Pensions, no. 10. Paris: OECD Publishing. https://doi.org/10.1787/5kg58j1lwdjd-en

Department of Forestry, Fisheries and the Environment (DFFE) and the National Treasury. 2022. "Republic of South Africa." *Technical Handbook on Issuing Municipal Sustainable Bonds in South Africa*. https://www.undp.org/sites/g/files/zskgke326/files/202208/Final%20Technical%20Handbook%20on%20Issuing%20Municipal%20Sustainable%20Bonds%20in%20South%20Africa.pdf.

Deschryver, Pauline, and Frederic de Mariz. 2020. "What Future for the Green Bond Market? How Can Policymakers, Companies, and Investors Unlock the Potential of the Green Bond Market?." *Journal of Risk and Financial Management* 13 (3): 61. https://doi.org/10.3390/jrfm13030061.

Egwu, C., P. Obasi, and J. Ogbonna. 2025. "Green Bond and Sustainable Infrastructure Development in Nigeria." *IOSR Journal of Business and Management* 16 (5, Series I): 31–38. https://doi.org/10.9790/5933-1605013138.

MCB Group. 2024. *Environmental and Cultural Heritage—MCB Group Sustainability Report 2024.* MCB Group. https://mcbgroup.com/docs/default-source/sustainability/report-2024/environmental-cultural-heritage.pdf.

Eron, Nanyonjo Grace. 2014. "Realizing Uganda's Energy Transition Plan: How Financial Institutions Can Facilitate Sustainable, Financing to Achieve a Just Transition." UBA Research Department. https://ugandabankers.org/wpcontent/uploads/2024/12/Realising-Energy-Transition-Plan-UBA-WP.pdf.

Farag, Noran, and Nadejda Komendantova. 2014. "Multiplier Effects on Socioeconomic Development from Investment in Renewable Energy Projects in Egypt: Desertec versus Energy for Local Consumption Scenarios." *International Journal of Renewable Energy Research* 4 (4).

Fatica, Serena, Roberto Panzica, and Michela Rancan. 2021. "The Pricing of Green Bonds: Are Financial Institutions Special?." *Journal of Financial Stability* 54: 100873. https://doi.org/10.1016/j.jfs.2021.100873.

FSDAfrica. 2025. *Green Bond Report: Final Report, March 20, 2025.* FSDAfrica. Accessed November 14, 2025. https://fsdafrica.org/wp-content/uploads/2025/05/Green-Bond-Report_Final-report-20.03.2025.pdf

FSDAfrica. 2025. *Impact of Green Bonds in Africa.* FSDAfrica. https://fsdafrica.org/wp-content/uploads/2025/05/Green-Bond-Report_Final-report-20.03.2025.pdf.

Global Green Growth Institute (GGGI). 2022. "Uganda Country Planning Framework." https://gggi.org/wp-content/uploads/2022/11/UGANDA-COUNTRY-PLANNING-FRAMEWORK-2022-2027.pdf, 2022–2027.

Green Bond Impact Report 2020. Bank Windhoek. https://www.bankwindhoek.com.na/Reports/2020%20Bank%20Windhoek%20Green%20Bond%20Impact%20Report%20(4MB).pdf.

Guesmi, Khaled, Panagiota Makrychoriti, and Emmanouil G. Pyrgiotakis. 2025. "Climate Change Exposure and Green Bonds Issuance." *Journal of International Money and Finance* 152: 103281. https://doi.org/10.1016/j.jimonfin.2025.103281.

Hadaś-Dyduch, Monika, Blandyna Puszer, Maria Czech, and Janusz Cichy. 2022. "Green Bonds as an Instrument for Financing Ecological Investments in the V4 Countries." *Sustainability* 14 (19): 12188. https://doi.org/10.3390/su141912188.

Hans, Verolme. 2021. Uganda Country Report-Climate Finance Pathfinder. https://doi.org/10.13140/RG.2.2.35345.86886.

ICMA. 2025. *Guidance on Allocation Reporting*. https://www.icmagroup.org/assets/documents/Sustainable-finance/2025-updates/Guidance-on-Allocation-Reporting-June-2025.pdf

International Finance Corporation (IFC). 2022. Emerging Market Green Bonds Report 2021. https://www.ifc.org/content/dam/ifc/doc/mgrt/202206-emerging-market-green-bonds-report-2021-vf-2.pdf.

Khan, Muhammad A., and Silvio Vismara. 2025. "Green Bond Issuance and Corporate Environmental and Financial Performance: A Meta-analysis." *International Review of Economics and Finance* 102: 104313. https://doi.org/10.1016/j.iref.2025.104313.

Kılıç, Arınç Onat. 2024. "Seychelles Blue Bond: Indebting Ecological Restructuring of Fisheries." *Marine Policy* 163: 106144. https://doi.org/10.1016/j.marpol.2024.106144.

Liu, Zehao, and Chi Paan. 2024. "Newly Evidence across the World on How Climate Financing Helps in Ensuring a Greener Future." *Heliyon* 10 (14): e34779. https://doi.org/10.1016/j.heliyon.2024.e34779.

Lukoye, Demas Kutosi, Amos Sanday, Victoria Kakooza, and Clet Wandui Masiga. 2025 ISSN 1916-971X e-ISSN 1916-9728. "Determinants of Interest Rate Spread: Empirical Evidence from Uganda's Banking Sector." *International Journal of Economics and Finance* 17 (4): 18. https://doi.org/10.5539/ijef.v17n4p18.

Ministry of Finance, Planning and Economic Development (MoFPED). 2024. *Guidelines for Mainstreaming Climate Action in the Financial Sector of Uganda.* Kampala: MoFPED. Accessed November 14, 2025. https://finance.go.ug/sites/default/files/reports/Guidelines%20for%20Mainstreaming%20Climate%20Action%20in%20the%20Financial%20Sector.pdf.

Ministry of Finance. 2025. "Planning and Economic Development (MOFPED)." *National Green Taxonomy (NGT).* https://finance.go.ug/sites/default/files/reports/National%20Green%20Taxonomy%202025.pdf.

Ministry of Water and Environment (MWE). 2022. *Updated Nationally Determined Contribution: Uganda.* Kampala: Ministry of Water and Environment. Accessed November 14, 2025. https://unfccc.int/sites/default/files/NDC/202209/Updated%20NDC%20_Uganda_2022%20Final.pdf.

Mohammed, A., and S. Zadek. 2018. *From Green Bonds to Sustainable Development the Case of Nigeria.*

Monaco, Salvatore. 2025. "The Other Side of Sustainability: Contradictions and Risks in Contemporary Green Innovations." *Sustainability* 17 (10): 4687. https://doi.org/10.3390/su17104687.

Napier, M., E. Osano, K. Munjal, J. Gathumi, J. Ampulire, C. Bjerborn Murai, J. Wanjiru et al., thank Kolapo.

National Planning Authority (NPA). 2020. "Third National." *Journal of Development Planning (NDPIII)* 2024/5. https://www.npa.go.ug/wp-content/uploads/2023/03/NDPIII-Finale_Compressed.pdf: 2020/21.

Ngwenya, Nomhle, and Mulala D. Simatele. 2020. "Unbundling of the Green Bond Market in the Economic Hubs of Africa: Case Study of Kenya, Nigeria and South Africa." *Development Southern Africa* 37 (6): 888–903. https://doi.org/10.1080/0376835X.2020.1725446.

Ntambirweki, B., A. Amumpiire, J. Okiira, S. Ong, R. Kaggwa, and A. Werikhe. 2022. "Enhancing Green Finance Access for Green Growth." *Policy Landscape Paper Uganda, Berlin, Germany*. https://www.acode-u.org/uploadedFiles/enhancing-green-finance-access-for-green-growth.pdf.

OECD (2025), Africa Capital Markets Report 2025, OECD Capital Market Series, OECD Publishing, Paris, https://doi.org/10.1787/7d26e1d3-en.

OECD. 2021. *Green Budget Tagging: Introductory Guidance & Principles*. Paris: OECD Publishing. https://doi.org/10.1787/fe7bfcc4-en.

Olakojo Yusuff Ogunsola, Yetunde Adenike Adebayo, Ikiomoworio Nicholas Dienagha, Nwakamma Ninduwezuor-Ehiobu, and Zamathula Sikhakhane Nwokediegwu. 2024. "Strategic Framework for Integrating Green Bonds and Other Financial Instruments in Renewable Energy Financing." *Gulf Journal of Advance Business Research* 2 (6): 461–472. https://doi.org/10.51594/gjabr.v2i6.59.

Otundo Richard, Martin. 2024. "Promoting Sustainable Growth: The Role of Natural Resource Utilization, Green Investment, Digital Finance, Industrial Usage, Energy

Efficiency, and Renewable Energy Consumption in Kenya, Rwanda and Uganda." *SSRN Electronic Journal*. https://doi.org/10.2139/ssrn.5015700.

Pava, M. O. 2024. "You Can Learn More about Our Work in Uganda." http://theigc.org/countries/uganda DIRECTED BY FUNDED BY Green finance in Uganda: Unlocking sustainable growth.

Peter, Malika. 2025. "Unlocking Domestic Finance through East Africa's First Subnational Green Bond." UN Capital Development Fund. https://www.uncdf.org/article/8920/unlocking-domestic-finance-through-east-africas-first-sub-national-green-bond.

Pointek, Thomas. 2025. "Fostering Capital Markets and Institutional Investor Development in Oman." *IMF Selected Issues Paper*. Washington, DC: International Monetary Fund 2025 (33): 1. https://doi.org/10.5089/9798229007917.018 (SIP. 2025/033).

Prisca, Wanyenya. 2025. "Uganda's Rising Debt Pile, Who Will Pay the UGX 116 Trillion Bill? Parliament Watch." https://parliamentwatch.ug/news-amp-updates/public-debt-hits-ugx116-trillion-mps-split-on-borrowing-appetite/.

Riaz, Tabassum, Aslam I. Selamat, Normaziah M. Nor, and Ahmad F. S. Hassan. 2025. "Do Investors Get an Advantage from Corporate Green Bond Issuance? A Cross-Country Study." *Studia Universitatis „ Vasile Goldis " Arad—Economics Series* 35 (2): 1–37. https://doi.org/10.2478/sues-2025-0006.

Rozkov, Deniss, and Hendrik Idema. 2023. "Institutional Investors' Preferences in Green Bonds and ESG Criteria: A Focus on German-Speaking Europe." *Managing Global Transitions* 21 (2). https://doi.org/10.26493/1854-6935.21.149-169.

Rusera, S., and J. J. Nsano. 2023. "Green Bond Framework, Prime Energy, Rukarara VI HPP." https://primeenergyltd.com/wp-content/uploads/2024/04/2024.03.06-_-Prime-Energy-_-Green-Bond-Framework.pdf.

Sajid, Muhammad J., Y. Zhang, and Laeeq R. Janjua. 2024. "Breaking Barriers: Assessing Technology Transfer for Climate-Resilient Development." *Environmental Technology and Innovation* 33: 103471. https://doi.org/10.1016/j.eti.2023.103471.

Simionescu, Mihaela, Magdalena Radulescu, and Lucian Belascu. 2024. "The Impact of Renewable Energy Consumption and Energy Poverty on Pollution in Central and Eastern European Countries." *Renewable Energy* 236: 121397. https://doi.org/10.1016/j.renene.2024.121397.

Sneideriene, Agne, and Renata Legenzova. 2025. "Greenwashing Prevention in Environmental, Social, and Governance (ESG) Disclosures: A Bibliometric Analysis." *Research in International Business and Finance* 74: 102720. https://doi.org/10.1016/j.ribaf.2024.102720.

Sun, Yiqun, and Y. Hao. 2025. "Green Bonds and Corporate Environmental Performance: The Role of Third-Party Certification." *International Review of Economics and Finance* 104: 104621. https://doi.org/10.1016/j.iref.2025.104621.

Sustainable Finance Initiative (SFI). 2021. *Success of East Africa's Debut Green Bond Issue: The Case of Acorn Holdings.* Nairobi: Sustainable Finance Initiative. Accessed November 14, 2025. https://sfi.kba.co.ke/uploads/case-studies/pdf/Acorn%20Holdings%20-%20Green%20Bond%20Issuance%20Case%20Study.pdf.

Uganda Bankers Association (UBA), 2024, Banking on a Green Future: How can Ugandan banks address climate-related risks and opportunities? https://ugandabankers.org/EY%20-%20Whitepaper%20-%20Banking%20on%20a%20Green%20Future.pdf

Wongaree, Parath, Chiraphol N. Chiyachantana, David K. Ding, Pattarawan Prasarnphanich, and Wasin Siwasarit. 2025. "The Pricing of Green Bonds and the Determinants of the Green Bond Premium in the Asia-Pacific and European

Markets." *Journal of Open Innovation: Technology, Market, and Complexity* 11 (2): 100546. https://doi.org/10.1016/j.joitmc.2025.100546.

Yu, Zhichao, Umar Farooq, Mohammad M. Alam, and Jiapeng Dai. 2024. "How Does Environmental, Social, and Governance (ESG) Performance Determine Investment mix? New Empirical Evidence from BRICS." *Borsa Istanbul Review* 24 (3): 520–529. https://doi.org/10.1016/j.bir.2024.02.007.

Zadek, Simon. 2018. "Financing a Just Transition." *Organization and Environment* 32 (1): 18–25. https://doi.org/10.1177/1086026618794176.

Zakari, Rafael Alvarado, Vincent Tawiah. 2022, "The Green Bond Market and Its Use for Energy Efficiency Finance in Africa." *China Finance Review International* 12 (2): 241–260. https://doi.org/10.1108/CFRI-12-2021-0225.

Zhang, Zihan. 2024. "The Development of Green Bonds: Current Issues and Solutions." *Highlights in Business, Economics and Management* 24: 722–730. https://doi.org/10.54097/3mfb8p84.

www.ingramcontent.com/pod-product-compliance
Lightning Source LLC
LaVergne TN
LVHW051131210926
848482LV00001B/66